ELECTIVE AFFINITIES

Private Collectors
& Special Collections in Libraries

ALICE D. SCHREYER

THE UNIVERSITY OF CHICAGO LIBRARY 2001

Published with the support of
the University of Chicago Library Society.

This talk was presented to
the University of Chicago Library Society
on October 10, 2001.
It was first delivered, in slightly different form, at
the Library of Congress Rare Book Forum
on April 4, 2001.

©2001 Alice Schreyer
For information contact:
The University of Chicago Library
1100 East 57th Street, Chicago, Illinois 60637
www.lib.uchicago.edu/e/spcl/

Design and typesetting by Lynn Martin.
Production editor Valarie Brocato.
Printed by Dupli-Graphic, Chicago, Illinois.
3,000 copies printed September 2001.

ISBN: 0-943056-29-2

PREFACE

In the following essay, Alice Schreyer pays tribute to book collectors and the vital role they have played in the development of research libraries in the United States. Ms. Schreyer's account draws on examples from a wide range of institutions; as she notes, the history of the University of Chicago Library testifies to the influence of private collectors. Characterizing the rare book community as an ecosystem in which changing environmental factors have affected relations among collectors, booksellers, scholars, and librarians, Ms. Schreyer describes the evolution of this ecosystem and provides perspectives for the future. Ms. Schreyer creates a candid and vivid impression of the sometimes conflicting expectations, personalities, values, and goals of the members of this community.

There is some irony in the fact that modern information technology, with its seemingly disembodied information represented in electronic impulses, is providing powerful access to special collections, which are so closely associated with physical artifacts. Information technology greatly increases the visibility of these original sources and makes them more readily available to a much wider audience. Ms. Schreyer's observations about the complex ways that information technology is affecting the book collecting ecosystem are particularly astute.

When I first read the manuscript of this essay, I had the urge to share it with others—certain that they too would find it insightful, instructive, and even inspiring. Subsequent rereading strengthened the urge. It is a privilege to present it to you in this handsome publication.

MARTIN D. RUNKLE
Director, The University of Chicago Library

Anniversaries are a time for reflection as well as celebration. Looking back on my first ten years as Curator of Special Collections, I recall the great joy of learning about and meeting the collectors and donors who helped to make the University of Chicago Library one of the world's great research libraries. Frank Wakeley Gunsaulus, Emma Hodge, Shirley Farr, Harold Swift and members of the Swift family are among the early donors featured in the current exhibition. Many of us had the privilege of knowing Joseph Halle Schaffner, Ludwig Rosenberger and Louis Szathmary. Several collector-donors are here tonight, and I hope others in the room will join their ranks in the future. Some were alumni, loyal Hyde Parkers or Chicagoans with strong ties to the University and its faculty or administration, others simply felt this was the best home for their collection. Their gifts to the University of Chicago were acts of great faith as well as generosity, for collectors are entrusting a most cherished possession to the stewardship of an institution. I take it as my chief responsibility to honor this trust and ensure that gift collections are properly maintained and fulfill the collector's vision of its educational and scholarly purpose.

I could easily fill our time this evening with the stories of remarkable gifts from private collectors to the University of Chicago Library, and indeed I hope to do that sometime in the future. The account would confirm and clarify our shared belief that this University, and its Library, are unique among its peers. But I have a different purpose in mind tonight. It seems appropriate on this occasion to look at relationships between private collectors and special collections in libraries from a broader perspective. What has been the role of private collectors in shaping American research libraries in the past, and what can we expect in the future? I am delighted to have the chance to share my thoughts on these important questions with you.

Fifty years ago, Louis B. Wright observed that "The United States owes a vast debt to book collectors, a debt far greater than the average citizen realizes."[1]

This admittedly obscure item in our national debt is not merely a matter of numbers. As I aim to illustrate, gifts from private collectors account for much of the depth, diversity, individuality—and quirkiness—of our nation's libraries. In addition, the efforts of private collectors have preserved parts of our national heritage that otherwise might have been lost, but are now available in research institutions. Special collections in libraries, and the issues facing them today, can only be understood in the context of the role played by private collectors in shaping them.[2] Spending public funds or student tuition on specialized materials has long been perceived as elitist, even dangerously undemocratic, as the debates in Congress over the purchase of Thomas Jefferson's library to replace the one burned by the British in the War of 1812 revealed.[3] Consequently, with a few notable exceptions, it has largely been private collectors who filled American libraries with rare and unique materials that are a national pride and a global resource.

The impact of private collectors on special collections in libraries goes well beyond the books and manuscripts they donated. They are responsible for the very look and feel of many of our libraries—free-standing buildings and elegantly appointed "rooms of one's own." Collectors also have influenced how libraries organize, preserve, interpret, promote and develop special collections. And perhaps most important, although hardest to document, is their contribution to teaching and research. It is often said that "libraries tend to reflect rather than create intellectual trends."[4] But private collectors are not obligated to meet curricular needs, or daunted by fugitive and fragile materials that are difficult for libraries to acquire and manage. Comprehensive collections formed by collectors and donated to libraries have extraordinary capacity to provoke scholars in new directions.

We can begin to repay our national debt through recognition and engagement, a task I view as one of environmental protection. As developed at the end of the nineteenth century by University of Chicago botanists, ecology studies environmental factors and relations between plants and animals that form one community.[5] The rare book community comprises several species—collector, bookseller, scholar and librarian—with different expectations, personalities, values and goals. Environmental factors that affect our community, such as trends in the economy, culture, higher education, technology, tax laws and philanthropy, are now in a particularly volatile state. There are strong indications that the culture of collecting is in transition, and we cannot presume that collections being formed today will be given to libraries in the future, as so many were in the past. It is also apparent that changes in libraries resulting from information technology will increase the importance of private collectors in maintaining the quality of research libraries. The past may hold clues to preserving the robustness of our ecosystem.

I will look at three periods in the last century when relationships between private collectors and special collections in libraries were affected by cultural, educational and economic changes. The first phase begins in the final decades of the nineteenth century, with the rise of research universities and a so-called golden age of book collecting. During this period, many private collections found their way back to the market; and libraries were only beginning to develop active programs to encourage gifts and manage special collections. In the post-war decades, the second era, the balance shifted dramatically. These years were characterized by a remarkable congruence of factors that stimulated gifts from private collectors and encouraged the development of special collections in libraries. The third phase brings us to the end of the twentieth century and provides perspectives for the future. In mapping it, I will be looking at changes in libraries in general and special collections in particular, alongside environmental factors that are altering relationships between private collectors and libraries.

A ROOM OF ONE'S OWN

Recognizing that students and citizens need libraries with scholarly and original sources to support research is a necessary precursor to developing special collections. This concept emerged late, although starting with John Harvard's 1638 gift of his books to the institution that bears his name, many private collectors established and enriched academic and public institutions. In fact, "For the first century and more of its existence, the [Harvard] library was dependent for its growth upon gifts."[6] James Logan's library, the largest in colonial America, was presented to the city of Philadelphia "for the public good" and is preserved in the Library Company of Philadelphia. Thomas Jefferson spent his last years forming a third collection of books that he intended for the University of Virginia and helping to build its library by encouraging gifts and recommending purchases. George Ticknor, impressed by European library resources he saw as a student abroad, was instrumental in founding the Boston Public Library, which opened in 1854. In 1895, prompted by the bequest of Samuel Tilden, the collections of John Jacob Astor and James Lenox were merged to form the New York Public Library's research division.[7]

In the final decades of the nineteenth century, Harvard and several other leading universities, including newcomers such as the University of Chicago, began in earnest to develop research collections.[8] University and public libraries grew rapidly during the first decades of the twentieth century, with the emphasis on acquiring current scholarly publications; scholars continued to head for Europe in search of original sources.[9]

These were years in which individuals were building great private collections—spurred by prosperity, ambition, extraordinary materials available from Europe in the wake of World War I, and a generation of brilliant and forceful booksellers exemplified by Dr. A. S. W. Rosenbach. E. D. Church's library was sold en bloc to Henry Huntington, but most—among them the Robert Hoe, Beverly Chew, Herschel V. Jones, Jerome Kern and John Quinn collections—were dispersed at auctions for record-breaking prices or sold back to dealers who had helped to build them.

What accounted for the assumption that a collection would be returned to the market? Many were high-spot collections not formed for scholarly purposes, and keeping rarities in circulation to give other collectors a chance at the joy of ownership is a recurring rationale for dispersal. Investment may not have been the primary motive for collecting, but a very strong market was certainly a strong temptation to sell. So, too, was the absence of incentives for giving. There was no deduction for charitable contributions in the original income tax act of 1913, although one was introduced in 1917. Over the years, this benefit was substantially extended, especially by the provision that the fair market value at the time of gift formed the basis for the deduction, and, of course, by soaring tax rates.[10]

Even more important than the lack of financial incentive was the fact that libraries made few efforts to attract collectors. As prices rose, libraries provided secure conditions for valuable materials that had been acquired—at older universities, often as new publications. Rare books were removed to locked cases in the director's office or "treasure rooms" for protection, with little attention to accessibility or use.[11] In fact, several prominent collectors expressed fear that their books would be buried or forgotten in a library. The neurosurgeon-medical history collector Harvey Cushing, speaking at the dedication of the William H. Welch Medical Library at Johns Hopkins in 1929, remarked, "Too often libraries are but the graveyard of forgotten books."[12]

What motivated the collectors of this era who decided to preserve their books in an institution? Was a library building just a different type of "monument" to their achievement than a sale catalog? Most well known are three who formed independent research libraries. J. Pierpont Morgan's collection was turned over by his son to the state of New York as a public reference library in 1924; Henry E. Huntington's library and art museum opened in San Marino in 1927, with an endowment for a research staff, fellowships and publications.[13] Henry Clay Folger provided for an active scholarly community at his library, the cornerstone for which was laid in 1930, two weeks before the donor's death.[14] Such arrangements suggest that these donors were not erecting mausoleums for their books, but fulfilling philanthropic goals and a desire to shape how their collections would be used in the future.

A number of prominent collectors who donated their libraries to academic institutions in the first decades of the twentieth century show a striking similarity in purpose and strategy to those who founded independent libraries. Institutional and civic loyalty, combined with a wish to make the collection available for educational purposes or research, was their chief intent. Although they wanted the stability and support of an existing institution, they also demanded independence from other library collections. Appropriate housing was crucial, but the physical space was designed principally to preserve the integrity of the collection and convey the donor's stature.

Alfred Chapin, a New York lawyer and politician, was inspired by his belief that contact with early editions and manuscripts would enrich an undergraduate liberal arts education.[15] His hopes were amply realized when the Chapin Library opened at Williams College in 1923. One of the first students to come into contact with the collection was William A. Jackson, who had been advised to attend Williams so that he could work with Chapin's books.[16]

Two other collectors followed the model of John Carter Brown, who established a separately administered library located at Brown University in 1901. William L. Clements and William Andrews Clark wanted to provide original research materials for advanced scholars, not a teaching collection for undergraduates. When Clements presented his Americana collection to his alma mater, Michigan, fellow regents, the university librarian and faculty all questioned the value of "a library devoted to one subject (broad though it was) and consisting primarily of rarities not for student use."[17] In his remarks at the 1923 dedication, Clements emphasized that "It is primarily a library for advanced research on the part of scholars already well equipped, rather than a library to serve as a vehicle of instruction for either the undergraduate or the ordinary graduate student."[18] This philosophy was characteristic of special collections in libraries for nearly another half-century.

William A. Clark, Jr. formed a similar plan. His collections of seventeenth- and eighteenth-century English books, Oscar Wilde and fine printing were housed in a library erected on his property in 1926. That same year he announced to the Board of Regents of the University of California that he was donating his collection and library "[to be used] by students for research work."[19] Clark set a number of conditions, prohibiting books leaving the building and erecting any other building within 180 feet of the Library. The Clark Library is now administered by UCLA's Center for Seventeenth and Eighteenth Century Studies, and a substantial endowment provides support for collection growth, fellowships and other activities.[20]

Not surprisingly, Harvey Cushing's concerns about the fate of books in libraries, expressed at Hopkins in 1929, shaped his negotiations with Yale about the gift of his collection. Cushing conceived an historical research center for humanistic studies in medicine and science, based on the model of the Osler library at McGill.[21] His arrangements also illustrate the magnetic force of gifts: Cushing persuaded two friends (Arnold Klebs and John F. Fulton) to combine their libraries with his and avoid duplication in their purchasing. He set as a condition that Yale provide a suitable building for the collection. When the start of World War II caused hesitation, Cushing threatened to give his collection elsewhere, but plans for a wing attached to the School of Medicine were confirmed just before Cushing's death in 1939. (He died of a heart attack brought on by lifting his folio Vesalius.)[22]

Timing is everything in gifts as in life. When Tracy McGregor visited Charlottesville shortly before his death, he concluded that the University of Virginia had the potential to become an important center for Americana research; and the trustees of the McGregor Fund carried out what they felt to be his intentions by presenting his collection and an endowment to Virginia. The gift arrived in the late-1930s, just after the opening of Alderman Library, and helped to solidify the institution's commitment to expanding research resources.[23]

Several factors at work in the inter-war years shifted the balance toward gifts to libraries. Selling a collection certainly lost its luster during the depression. And institutions stepped up efforts to develop new collectors and to cultivate collectors as donors. Booksellers have always understood that encouraging new collectors is essential to their business prospects, and they invest substantial effort in forming relationships and offering expert advice. The emergence of library cultivation depended on the appointment of curators with the knowledge and interest to build connections with collectors and educate new ones, especially students who would become loyal alumni. George Parker Winship, who taught "The History of the Printed Book," better known as Fine Arts 5e, at Harvard from 1915 to 1932, initiated a select band of undergraduates into connoisseurship and collecting with the expressed intention of developing future donors to Harvard.[24] Arthur Houghton and Philip Hofer are only two examples of his success. At Yale, Chauncey Brewster Tinker, the great scholar-collector who was appointed Keeper of Rare Books when Sterling Memorial Library opened in 1930, launched the Yale Library Associates as part of his effort to attract gifts of collections and separate funds for the purchase of special materials.[25] As friends groups were founded, they provided a venue for developing relationships with private collectors and created opportunities for collectors to become involved with the institution and learn about its strengths and needs. Curators (nearly all of them male at this time) took advantage of membership in book collecting clubs such as Grolier, Caxton and Rowfant to interact with private collectors. By the time Seymour de Ricci published his *Census of Medieval and Renaissance Manuscripts in the United States and Canada* in the mid-1930s, he defended his decision to include private collections as follows: "in the United States and Canada, private ownership of early manuscripts is essentially a transitory feature of book-collecting. Nearly all valuable manuscripts in private hands are destined in the near future to become public property."[26]

But trustees and academic administrators continued to question the expenditure of funds to purchase or maintain special collections. The tension surfaced at Harvard in the late 1930s over the appointment by Keyes Metcalf of William A. Jackson as Associate Professor of Bibliography and Assistant Librarian in charge of the rare book collection, and the need for more space and better environmental conditions than those provided in Widener. Charles Warren, the constitutional lawyer who chaired the Library's Visiting Committee, "felt that the University had no business acquiring and caring for rare books and manuscripts, and that a librarian to look after such things was certainly not needed."[27] Arthur Houghton immediately stepped in with a gift to build the Houghton Library, which opened in 1942.

Gifts by private collectors to public institutions are often explicit acts of local or national pride and personal gratitude. This is certainly true of Dr. Albert A. Berg and Lessing Rosenwald, both of whom continued to build their collections long after they had been given away. Berg and his brother Henry had worked in the library of Cooper Union and formed an early love of English and American literature.[28] They offered their collection to the New York Public Library on the condition that the books be housed in a separate room. According to John Gordan, founding Berg curator, "This generous offer put the Board of Trustees in a quandary, because space is almost the most precious thing in a library today" (he was writing in 1954).[29] Within fifteen months after Dr. Albert A. Berg made the gift in 1940 (after Henry's death), the collection was increased by ten times its original size; and a generous endowment provides for continued growth.

Lessing Rosenwald occupies a special place in any survey of philanthropy and cultural history. Rosenwald began collecting early printed and illustrated books in the mid-1920s. He presented approximately 400 volumes to the Library of Congress in 1943, and by 1978 the collection had grown to more than 2,600 separate editions and 5,000 reference volumes. The Library was encouraged to dispose of duplicates from the collection when it had a superior copy and use the funds for needed acquisitions. During Rosenwald's lifetime the collection remained in Jenkintown, Pennsylvania; it is now housed in the Rosenwald Room, in the Library's Jefferson Building, with the furniture from Alverthorpe.[30] Frederick Goff remarked that "Since its founding in 1800, no donor to the Library of Congress has been more generous than Lessing Rosenwald," high praise indeed in view of the many great gifts to the Library of Congress, but surely no exaggeration.[31]

A GOLDEN AGE FOR GIFTS

The post-war decades, which constitute the second phase of my overview, were a period of economic prosperity, inflation, and ambitious and rapid institutional growth. These factors were extremely favorable for gifts and also made libraries a powerful force in the rare book market. In a rush to build institutional reputations and library collections, academic administrators provided funding for large-scale, en bloc purchases, even arguing that public funds should be allocated to rare books and manuscripts. The Humanities Research Center, founded in 1957 by Harry Ransom, then provost and later president and chancellor at the University of Texas, Austin, is the most spectacular and well-known example. Ransom's purchase of the T. E. Hanley library set the course for future acquisitions focusing on twentieth-century literature and inaugurated the institution's dramatic impact on the market for modern literary manuscripts.[32] The alliance between chancellor Franklin Murphy and university librarian Lawrence Clark Powell enabled UCLA to purchase Michael Sadleir's novels and many other collections.

Gordon Ray analyzed the phenomenon in a 1978 essay: "In the process of serving as centers of scholarship, American libraries since the end of the Second World War have turned the book-collecting world upside down, imposing scarcity where was once abundance. The upshot has been an almost exponential rise in the price of antiquarian books in nearly every conceivable collecting field.... As long as gifts to non-profit institutions were fully tax deductible, an uneasy alliance prevailed between collectors and libraries."[33]

In spite of—or more likely as a result of—this shared acquisitorial zeal, relationships between collectors and librarians flourished in the post-war decades. Curators of this generation, from backgrounds as diverse as academe and the booktrade—James T. Babb and Herman (Fritz) Liebert at Yale; Lilly's first librarian, David Randall, and his successor, Bill Cagle; Robert Rosenthal at Chicago; Lawrence Towner at the Newberry; Kenneth Lohf at Columbia; the Library Company of Philadelphia's Edwin Wolf 2nd—constituted a unique breed of grand collection-builders. Their passion to build collections created natural affinities with private collectors, and they formed close ties with many who were their benefactors. Dealers, too, joined the ranks of donors, among them Rosenbach, Bernardo Mendel, Hans Kraus and Michael Papantonio. Perhaps for once, the egos of collectors, dealers and librarians were evenly matched.

This was also a time for formalizing special collections programs in libraries. Administrative units established to maintain consolidated collections of rare books and manuscripts were often called "special collections" departments in order to signal the broadened scope and de-emphasize the "treasures" model that had focused on rarity alone.[34] Library friends groups, a number of which had lapsed, were revived or formed to organize lectures, exhibition openings and other events, drawing collectors and donors together in scholarly and bibliophilic fellowship. The longstanding tradition of recognizing gift collections and endowed funds with bookplates was expanded to encompass exhibitions, catalogs and other activities to acknowledge and publicize gifts.

Separate physical space helped libraries to create a distinct identity for these new programs and fulfilled donors' continuing desires to preserve the integrity and separateness of their collections. Examples of special rooms abound, for example the one designed for James Ford Bell's collection of travel literature at the University of Minnesota; several at Princeton's Firestone Library, including rooms for the Scheide and Robert Taylor libraries; the Elkins room at the Free Library of Philadelphia. And even when there was no obligation to create or recreate the ambiance of a private library, institutions often designed them on their own. When the Joseph Regenstein Library was planned in the mid-1960s, the Department of Special Collections was designed with a wood-paneled exhibition gallery and bookcase-lined alcoves at obvious odds with the modernist aesthetic prevailing elsewhere in the building. The Rosenberger Room, added in the early 1980s, replicates the environment in which Ludwig Rosenberger's library was housed in his office. The museum function in libraries is an uneasy fit, since books, unlike works of art, are made to be handled by readers and not viewed as objects. But rare books on permanent display and in exhibition cases are more than a decorating scheme. They send a strong message to visitors, among them potential donors, that the library prizes these collections, treats them with special distinction and announces their availability to prospective users.

Josiah Lilly's gift of his collection, ranging across great works of literature, science and Americana, exemplifies the forces that drew private collectors and libraries together during this period. Lilly apparently never set foot on the campus before he decided to give his collection to Indiana University. Hoosier loyalty and favorable tax laws were essential factors in the gift, but President Herman B. Wells created the necessary environment. Wells, like Franklin Murphy at UCLA and Harry Ransom at Texas, understood the importance of an outstanding library as a magnet for scholars and a means to raise the stature of a state institution. The Lilly Library building, dedicated in 1960, was financed by public bonds and depends on funds from the university library for staff and maintenance expenditures. This situation illustrates the challenge posed by unendowed operational costs for a freestanding rare book library at a public institution, especially when the financial circumstances become more constrained.[35]

The University of Virginia has long enjoyed the benefits of generous private collectors and strong institutional support. C. Waller Barrett's collecting scope is legendary—175 years of American literature, from 1775 to 1950, encompassing works of minor as well as major figures in all genres. Barrett continued to collect after he made his first gift in 1946 until his death in 1991, although he excluded William Faulkner because Linton Massey was forming his Faulkner collection, also now at Virginia. The beautiful and meticulous French Renaissance and Enlightenment books collected by Douglas Gordon appear quite out of the mainstream of Virginia's Americanist collecting focus, but they too have attracted substantial interest from researchers, confirming the potential of special collections to attract new constituencies. Gordon set the condition that if any books are displayed opened, the collection will go to Harvard (after all, he was a Fine Arts 5e alumnus). Recently, Virginia received part of Paul Mellon's collection, which was divided according to a plan facilitated by bookseller William S. Reese. Each of three institutions (Yale and Virginia Historical Society were the other two) identified the materials that were of the highest priority for its collection. Virginia is now building the Albert Small Special Collections Library, actively supported by President John Casteen, whose own experience working as a student in special collections inspired abiding interest.[36]

A collection that flourished on soil needing careful cultivation is the library of Rachel McMasters Miller Hunt.[37] Mrs. Hunt regularly lectured in conjunction with exhibitions from her collection, and she was approached by many institutions when considering its disposition. But she and her husband were fiercely loyal to Pittsburgh, where they had acquired their wealth, and determined to raise its stature as a cultural and intellectual center. Carnegie Institute had no botany or plant science collections, no history of science programs and no place to put the collection. The Hunt Botanical Library was presented to the Carnegie Institute of Technology in 1961 and remains administratively separate from the library. It is housed in surroundings that evoke the magnificence of Mrs. Hunt's home library, even though her warning to her husband Roy, the head of the Aluminum Company of America, that she didn't "want any aluminum in my Penthouse!" went unheeded.[38] First with support from the Hunt family and then a one-time endowment gift from the Hunt Foundation, the Library (renamed the Hunt Institute for Botanical Documentation in 1970) promotes the scholarly activity that Mrs. Hunt wanted her books to sustain.[39]

Even when collectors do not fund or require a new library or wing as a condition of their gift, they can have a "construct"-ive effect on institutional facilities. Everett Graff, a Chicagoan who collected Western Americana with the help of dealer Wright Howes, used his potential gifts as a "stick" to encourage needed physical improvements.[40] He persuaded the Art Institute to renovate its building and used a similar strategy at the Newberry Library, where he gave and bequeathed his 10,000 books. Graff decided early on that his books would go to the Newberry because of its existing strength in his field of interest, and he consciously built his collection as a complement to Edward Ayer's North American Indian Collection.[41]

Buying with the express intention that the books will go to a particular institution, as Barrett and Graff did, is one way to avoid direct competition. In a talk read by his son at the Clark Library shortly before his death in 1976, Yale's illustrious James Osborne acknowledged the potential for competition between collectors and libraries. He cautioned collectors to be alert to collecting in one's field by libraries and "aware of how best to cooperate" rather than compete.[42]

When the collector is also the curator, the situation is even more delicate. As an undergraduate at Harvard and a student in Winship's Fine Arts 5e, Philip Hofer was already a well-developed book collector.[43] In 1938 Hofer was appointed founding curator of the Department of Printing and Graphic Arts, the first of its kind and built around Hofer's own collection.[44] Over the succeeding years, as described by Eleanor Garvey, "With a flexibility scarcely possible today, Hofer collected for the university and for himself, often a source of confusion when the materials were exhibited. His bequest of 1984 clarified the picture and the numbers.... He had, indeed, been collecting for Harvard."[45] As Garvey's comments suggest, libraries are increasingly uncomfortable when the lines between collector and curator are blurred. In fact, the code of professional ethics for special collections librarians—like the ethical standards for museum curators—specifically prohibits this potential conflict of interest. The shift is part of a trend toward businesslike practices and institutional accountability that characterized libraries in the last quarter of the twentieth century, to which I will now turn.

AN ERA OF ACCESS AND CHANGE

As economic pressures and information technology began to transform libraries in the 1970s, a generation of aggressive collection-building shifted to an emphasis on preservation and use. Expanding access to rare and unique materials has been a key focus of special collections programs for the past twenty-five years. Libraries have dedicated substantial resources, often assisted by external funds, to provide electronic information about collections, expand the visibility of special collections and, more recently, explore the potential of digital surrogates as adjuncts to original materials. As a result, entirely new audiences are finding special collections through Web-based catalogs and online presentations such as the Library of Congress's American Memory program. We are promoting use of primary sources—formerly reserved for advanced researchers—in undergraduate instruction and creating online collections for elementary and high school students. Fellowship programs to support visiting scholars are now common. "Blockbuster" library exhibitions and glossy publications are also designed to attract new audiences and broaden support.

Another phenomenon of the last quarter of the twentieth century is the professionalization of special collections librarianship. Educational programs such as the one established by Terry Belanger at Columbia's School of Library Service in the mid-1970s identified special collections as a separate field within librarianship, with its own body of knowledge and skills. Training centered on bibliographical expertise and book history within the framework of library-wide issues and operations.

These developments, which have greatly strengthened special collections programs in libraries, should also have fostered confidence on the part of collectors, who expect and respect responsible care and use of their books. Instead, there are indications that the stewardship role librarians are exercising, which contrasts sharply with the entrepreneurial spirit of collectors, is making communication more difficult. One bookseller, describing what he views as a serious rift, recently accused librarians of "becoming more like MBAs."[46] Are collectors attracted to the very aspects of special collections that led Neil Harris to suggest a decade ago that "rare book and special collections might be labelled as evocative atavisms"?[47] At the very least we have failed to convey to collectors the value, importance and excitement of these changes. Moving away from a marginalized position into the center of education, scholarship and libraries is the key to expanding broad appreciation and institutional support for special collections in libraries. As Louis Wright observed, "The conversion of a private collection into an operating library is not an easy process and sometimes collectors are not aware of the difficulties."[48] In the final section of my remarks I will look at specific issues causing tensions and suggest strategies for productive partnerships.

Providing access to rare books is a labor-intensive and costly process, and cataloging backlogs grew along with collections in the post-war years. Not all collectors are concerned with such details, and for some a printed catalog (which can be, like the Pforzheimer catalog of English literature, a work of enduring scholarly value) is far more important than library catalog records. But no collector wants to discover that a collection is untouched long after it was donated. Elisabeth Ball, who continued her father's interest in collecting children's literature, made gifts to several libraries. On a visit to the Morgan Library she was distressed to see much of her collection still in boxes.[49] The majority of her collection was given in 1983, after Miss Ball's death, by the George and Frances Ball Foundation to the Lilly Library.[50] The Lilly was able to provide detailed cataloging of the Ball collection with support from the National Endowment for the Humanities. In the 1980s and 1990s, NEH and other federal agencies funded many projects that added new records to online databases. These initiatives helped greatly to improve access to special collections in libraries, but such funding sources are now substantially reduced.

Special collections librarians have an obligation to raise vital, often delicate issues and broaden understanding of today's complex library environment without offending—or boring—collectors. Curators need to be skilled leaders and administrators, as well as passionate and knowledgeable about books, to secure support for their programs. This is one of many reasons for concern about reduced educational opportunities for special collections librarianship resulting from the closing of several library schools and the radical reshaping of the curriculum at others.

Developing special collections has always been opportunistic. We continue to exercise flexibility in "building on strength," but space and staff limitations, and commitment to preserve and provide access to what we add, require us to be more selective. Collectors who have been well informed about a library's program will understand a decision to decline an offer of out-of-scope materials. When a very welcome gift contains already-held items, we need to discuss options such as the sale of duplicates for funds to build the collection. And while deaccessioning can be an appropriate and responsible action under certain circumstances, who can deny that the publicity surrounding such incidents (as at Kansas City in the early 1990s) undermines faith in the integrity of collections donated to institutions?[51] Widely publicized thefts evoke concern over library security. We haven't found an easy way to talk about other areas, either. Space constraints make it far more difficult to accommodate a donor's desire for separate housing. We can use technology to preserve the intellectual integrity of a collection that has been physically dispersed, but for some this may not be enough. The solemn, sacred spaces we have built to please donors create environments that many students and members of the public find intimidating. And, increasingly, libraries must appeal to individual donors for support of operations such as processing and preservation. Librarians would be remiss not to explain what is needed to do justice to a collection, but no amount of diplomacy makes it easy to ask someone for money who has just offered you a magnificent collection.

    Collectors continue to transform institutions with the power of their gifts. Under directors Frederick B. Adams and Charles Ryskamp, the Morgan Library expanded well beyond the scope of the founder's collection, and current director Charles Pierce has taken the next steps toward building a "full-service" research library.[52] His effort is succeeding because the institution has gained the confidence and devotion of private collectors. Indeed if academic libraries are blessed in their alumni, independent and some public libraries have created chic and fashionable collectors' circles that foster comparable loyalty and the cachet of affiliation with a great institution.

Gordon Ray was one of the greatest scholar-collector-philanthropists of the second half of the twentieth century. He was also perhaps the keenest observer of relationships between libraries, scholars and collectors. The crucial factor in the disposition of his collections of English and French illustrated books, English and French literature, and mystery novels was Ray's close involvement with the Morgan, which enabled him to envision the potential to create an entirely new depth and range in an institution he knew so well.

Carter Burden's collection stretches the Morgan yet further in terms of scope and size. Burden described his original goal as "comprehensiveness and completeness" in the field of American literature from 1880 onward, "at least subconsciously" picking up where Waller Barrett left off.[53] He observed that "the market attaches no value whatsoever to comprehensiveness.... The payoff will come from future scholars, students, and readers, who use and depend upon our great university and research libraries where those collections ultimately belong."[54] The Burden collection will fulfill this vision at the Morgan Library, to which Mrs. Susan Burden presented the collection in 1999, three years after Burden's sudden death. The gift presents a number of challenges, the most obvious being space.

In June 2000, Lloyd Cotsen presented over 20,000 children's books to his alma mater, Princeton. Children's literature is not an area previously emphasized at Princeton, indeed it is a field that is still seeking full academic respectability. Mr. Cotsen set a number of stringent conditions regarding space, programs and publications, along with an endowment that made these requirements feasible. Community response is positive and faculty interest is building. At the same time, rapid collection growth is presenting storage problems; and while the printed collection catalogs will provide access, the holdings are not represented online and exceed the library's current cataloging capacity. Was Princeton the "right" institution for this collection? Was the institution "right" to accept it? Of course there are no easy or correct answers, especially to this work-in-progress, but it is already apparent that the Cotsen Children's Library will have a dramatic impact on the scholarly and public appreciation of literature for children.[55]

It is impossible to overstate the important role libraries play in bringing collectors into contact with kindred spirits—others involved with the history and art of collecting—and providing access to curatorial expertise. Special collections librarians struggling to balance multiple responsibilities may view long lunches with collectors or dinners at the Grolier Club a luxury, but personal contacts are the glue that holds our relationships together. And, just as booksellers recognize they need to work harder at developing new clients in the age of the Internet, librarians must continue cultivating future generations of collectors.[56] Courses such as Fine Arts 5e and presentations to students and visiting groups provide a chance to experience the excitement of interacting with rare books directly. Programs such as Rare Book School at the University of Virginia bring librarians, collectors, scholars and booksellers together to share intense learning experiences. Student book collecting contests, such as the Adrian VanSinderen Award that T. Kimball Brooker won at Yale and the prize he has endowed at the University of Chicago, are invaluable allies in fostering love of books, collecting and libraries.

In an article written for *The New Colophon* a half-century ago and still right on target, Randolph G. Adams posed the following questions for a book collector who announces that "I plan to leave my books to a library":

> *What library?*
> *Are you satisfied that the library of your choice will have any understanding of what you are giving?*
> *What is the record of that library with respect to such gifts?*
> *What do you know about the history of gifts and benefactions such as you propose?*

What are you doing to be sure that your books will be kept in the same condition they are now in?

Are you making conditions about the disposal of duplicates, and are you sure that anyone on the staff of the library of your choice knows a duplicate when he sees one?

Do you know that the library of your choice will service your books with due regard to bibliographical scholarship, physical care, and the needs of intelligent readers?

Do you care whether the librarian slings your books on open shelves or in stacks where they can easily be removed by nimble-fingered and migratory experts who will dispose of them with great anonymity and profit?

What provisions are you making for the expansion, growth, and evolution of your collection?[57]

As I have been suggesting, when a library is offered a gift by a private collector, it must also consider a series of questions. Here is how I would formulate them:

Will this collection promote institutional identity and distinctiveness?

Will this collection transform an existing good collection into a great one, or create strength where none existed?

Will this collection attract future gifts?

Will this collection support current scholarship; provide the basis for publications, lectures, fellowships and exhibitions; energize undergraduate and graduate teaching?

Will this collection stimulate new fields of research and promote public appreciation of books?

If this collection were split up by sale, would it make it difficult or impossible for certain types of scholarship to be done or would it make no difference to future research?

Is there another institution that is an obvious fit for this collection?

Will this collection facilitate faculty recruitment and retention?

Do we have adequate space to house it?

What is the percentage of materials truly needed for the collection, and what options do we have for the items not needed for the collection?

What will we need to stop doing or put aside to devote the necessary resources to this collection?

Do we have the staff to catalog it?

What preservation needs does it have and how will these be fulfilled?

Are the donor's expectations or conditions reasonable and appropriate, and do we have the resources to meet them?

Will we have funds to maintain and develop the collection?

Not surprisingly, the questions asked by private collectors and libraries both focus on:

Institutional mission
Institutional credibility
Staff resources for maintaining and enhancing the collection
Preservation of the collection
Disposition of duplicates
Bibliographic access
Use of the collection
Physical facilities and security
Continued development of the collection
Availability of properly educated and trained staff into the future.

These mutual interests create an "elective affinity" between private collectors and libraries, like the attraction between different chemical elements described by late eighteenth-century scientists. We need to acknowledge our different perspectives as well as our shared devotion to the rare book community and the culture of private collecting on which it depends, in order to strengthen the powerful bonds that draw us together.

Our current environment presents both opportunities and threats. Rare books and manuscripts are recognized more than ever before as central to the cultural and educational mission of universities and libraries, but increasing numbers of them seem headed back to the marketplace. Technology is introducing new audiences to special collections, but electronic information is also making libraries more homogeneous, because a growing percentage of the acquisitions budget in most institutions must be devoted to digital resources. As a result, retrospective and rare book collections will play a greater and far more visible role in creating institutional distinctiveness and individuality. Collectors will continue to preserve artifacts of our cultural heritage, especially contemporary materials, that libraries are not collecting because they do not meet current scholarly needs or as a result of funding limitations. As scholarship evolves and these materials become essential primary resources, private collectors will play a vital part in making them available.[58] Special collections hold the sources that set institutions apart from each other, preserve the personalities of our nation's libraries and create unique opportunities for scholarship and learning. In the future as in the past, private collectors will help to shape special collections in libraries.

In a classic study of gift-giving rituals in ancient and small-scale societies, the French scholar Marcel Mauss observed that a gift is an intimate part of the giver. According to Mauss, gifts confer responsibilities on the recipient to deepen the connection with the giver.[59] Although Mauss and other early writers believed that traditional gift-giving was lost in a modern, market economy, a broader view is now gaining acceptance.[60] Gifts by collectors to America's research libraries are certainly characterized by a number of the features described by Mauss. The magic, power and identity of collectors flow with their gifts. Libraries have an obligation to fulfill the conditions that come with a gift and to recognize it with tangible forms such as bookplates, catalogs and exhibitions. An institution creates a meaningful, enduring connection with a collector when it develops the gift as a foundation for preserving and fostering appreciation of our cultural heritage. This is how we repay our nation's debt to collector-donors and ensure that our libraries continue to benefit from their great generosity—through recognition and relationships that continue well beyond the actual gift-giving.

NOTES

1. "American Book Collectors," in *Book Collecting and Scholarship; Essays,* by Theodore C. Blegen [et al.] (Minneapolis: University of Minnesota Press, 1954), pp. 51-52.

2. I want to express warm thanks to the colleagues with whom I spoke while preparing this paper. Several of these exchanges are cited in subsequent notes. I am especially grateful to James M. Wells, Custodian Emeritus of the John M. Wing Collection in the History of Printing, Newberry Library, for sharing his keen observations on the rare book world so generously.

3. See Neil Harris, "Public Funding for Rarity: Some American Debates," *Libraries & Culture; A Journal of Library History* 31, no. 1 (1996): 36-55.

4. Phyllis Dain, "Scholarship, Higher Education, and Libraries in the United States: Historical Questions and Quests," in *Libraries and Scholarly Communication in the United States; The Historical Dimension,* ed. by Phyllis Dain and John Y. Cole (New York: Greenwood Press, 1990; Beta Phi Mu Monograph, No. 2), p. 16.

5. "The Origins of Ecology," University of Chicago American Environmental Photographs Collection, American Memory, Library of Congress. Aug. 2, 2001 <http://memory.loc.gov/ammem/award97/icuhtml/aepsp2.html>.

6. *Harvard University Library, 1638-1968* (Cambridge, Mass.: Harvard University Library, 1969), p. 10.

7. See Carl L. Cannon, *American Book Collectors and Collecting from Colonial Times to the Present* (New York: H.W. Wilson, 1941) for James Logan, pp. 26-37; Thomas Jefferson, pp. 38-49; George Ticknor,

pp. 57-63; and James Lenox, pp. 72-77. See also Harry Clemons, *The University of Virginia Library 1825-1950; Story of a Jeffersonian Foundation* (Charlottesville: University of Virginia Library, 1954), pp. 1-11; "At the Instance of Benjamin Franklin: A Brief History of the Library Company of Philadelphia," Library Company of Philadelphia. Aug. 2, 2001 <http://www.librarycompany.org/Instancedefault.htm>; Phyllis Dain, *The New York Public Library; A History of Its Founding and Early Years* (The New York Public Library, 1972), pp. 36-77; and Walter Muir Whitehill, *Boston Public Library; A Centennial History*, illus. by Rudolph Ruzicka (Cambridge, Mass.: Harvard University Press), pp. 1-42.

8. See Arthur T. Hamlin, *The University Library in the United States; Its Origins and Development* (Philadelphia: University of Pennsylvania Press, 1981), pp. 87-92.

9. See for example, Robert Vosper, "Books for Libraries: Institutional Book Collecting," in *Building Book Collections; Two Variations on a Theme. Papers Read at a Clark Library Seminar, February 7, 1976*, by James M. Osborn [and] Robert Vosper (Los Angeles: William Andrews Clark Memorial Library, 1977), pp. 22-23.

10. Edith L. Fish, Doris Jonas Freed [and] Esther R. Schachter, *Charities and Charitable Foundations* (Pomona, NY: Lond Publications, 1974), p. 624; William P. Barlow, Jr., "The Future of Rare Book and Manuscript Libraries and the Tax Laws," in *Rare Book and Manuscript Libraries in the Twenty-First Century*, ed. by Richard Wendorf (Cambridge, Mass.: Harvard University Library, 1993), pp. 100-106.

11. William L. Joyce, "Special Collections," in *Encyclopedia of Library History*, ed. by Wayne A. Wiegand and Donald G. Davis, Jr. (New York: Garland, 1994), pp. 595-97.

12. *The Binding Influence of a Library on a Subdividing Profession. An Address at the Dedication of the William H. Welch Medical Library of The Johns Hopkins University School of Medicine, October 17, 1929* (Baltimore, Md., 1930), pp. 29-30.

13. See *American Book Collectors and Collecting* for J. Pierpont Morgan, pp. 277-91; and Roland Baughman in *Grolier 75; A Biographical Retrospective to Celebrate the Seventy-Fifth Anniversary of the Grolier Club in New York* (New York: The Grolier Club, 1959) for Henry Huntington, pp. 58-60.

14. "American Book Collectors," pp. 54-62.

15. "History of the Chapin Library," Williams College. Aug. 2, 2001 <http://www.williams.edu/resources/chapin/History/history.html>. See also Lucy E. Osborne, "Rare Books in a College Program," *Library Journal* 66: 386-87; and H. Richard Archer, "The Chapin Library after Thirty-Five Years," *Quarterly News Letter of the Book Club of California* (Summer 1958): 51-57.

16. Roger E. Stoddard, "'Dear Lawrence,' 'Dear Bill': William A. Jackson, Lawrence C. Wroth, and the Practice of Bibliography in America," *PBSA* 94, no. 4 (2000): 484.

17. *History of the William L. Clements Library 1923-1973; Its Development and Collections* (Ann Arbor: The University of Michigan, 1973), p. 2.

18. Printed in *The American Historian's Raw Materials; An Address by J. Franklin Jameson. With the*

Presentation and Other Exercises at the Dedication of the William L. Clements Library of Americana (Ann Arbor: University of Michigan, 1923), pp. 13-14.

19. I am indebted to Bruce Whiteman, Librarian, The William Andrews Clark Memorial Library, for a copy of Clark's letter to the Regents, June 4, 1926, and for his information and observations. Telephone conversation, January 8, 2001.

20. Lawrence Clark Powell in *Grolier 75*, p. 199.

21. Lycurgus M. Davey, "Harvey Cushing and the Humanities in Medicine," *Journal of the History of Medicine* (April 1969): 121.

22. Ibid., p. 122.

23. Clemons, pp. 168-9. I am indebted to Kathryn Morgan, Associate Director of Special Collections, University of Virginia Library, for observations and information in this paragraph. Telephone conversation, January 16, 2001.

24. Roger Stoddard, quoted in Nicholas A. Basbanes, *A Gentle Madness; Bibliophiles, Bibliomanes, and the Eternal Passion for Books* (New York: Henry Holt, 1995), p. 193. See Michael Winship, "Fine Arts 5e: The Invention and the Aftermath," in *George Parker Winship as Librarian, Typophile and Teacher . . .* (Cambridge, Mass.: Harvard College Library, 1999), pp. 28-40.

25. Marjorie G. Wynne, *The Rare Book Collections at Yale; Recollections, 1942-1987 . . .* (New York: Columbia University, 1988; Book Arts Press Occasional Publication No. 5), pp. 13-14.

26. Quoted in Gregory A. Pass, "Electrifying Research in Medieval and Renaissance Manuscripts," *PBSA* 94, no. 4 (December 2000): 513.

27. "The Houghton Library: Notes on Its Origin and Development," *A Houghton Library Chronicle 1942-1992* (Cambridge, Mass.: Harvard College Library, 1992), p. 4.

28. John D. Gordan in *Grolier 75*, p. 188.

29. "A Doctor's Benefaction: The Berg Collection at The New York Public Library," *PBSA* 48 (Fourth Quarter, 1954): 305-306.

30. This summary is based on William Matheson, "Lessing J. Rosenwald; 'A Splendidly Generous Man,'" in *Vision of a Collector; The Lessing J. Rosenwald Collection in the Library of Congress* (Library of Congress, Rare Book and Special Collections Division, 1991), pp. xxiii-xxxiii.

31. Quoted by Helmut N. Friedlaender in *Grolier 2000; A Further Grolier Club Biographical Retrospective in Celebration of the Millennium* (New York: The Grolier Club, 2000), p. 320.

32. Thomas F. Staley in *Grolier 2000*, pp. 305-307; "History of the rare book and manuscript collections." Aug. 2, 2001 < http:// www.hrc.utexas.edu/books/bkframeset.html>.

33. "American Libraries as Centers of Scholarship: A Retrospective View," reprinted in *Books as a Way*

of Life; Essays (New York: The Grolier Club [&] The Pierpont Morgan Library, 1988), p. 317.

34. See Joyce, p. 597.

35. I am indebted to Lisa Browar for information and insights in this paragraph. Conversation and letters, January 5 and 18, 2001. See also Cecil K. Byrd, "Introduction: A Brief History," *The Lilly Library: The First Quarter Century 1960-1985* (Bloomington, IN: The Lilly Library, Indiana University, 1985), pp. 1-17.

36. Mary Cooper Gilliam in *Grolier 2000,* pp. 15-18; Kathryn Morgan; and University of Virginia Library web site. Aug. 2, 2001 <http://www.lib.virginia.edu/speccol/new/new.html> and <http://www.lib.virginia.edu/ speccol/colls/rarebooks.html>.

37. I am indebted to Charlotte Tancin, Librarian & Senior Research Scholar, Hunt Institute for Botanical Documentation, for information and insights in this paragraph. Telephone conversation, January 22, 2001.

38. George H.M. Lawrence, "Rachel McMasters Miller Hunt—1882-1963," *Huntia* 1 (1964): 5 and 7.

39. Ibid., p.15.

40. James M. Wells in *Grolier 2000,* p. 138.

41. Lawrence W. Towner, "A History of the Newberry Library," in *Humanities' Mirror; Reading at the Newberry, 1887-1987,* comp. and ed. by Rolf Achilles (Chicago: The Newberry Library, 1987), p. 19.

42. "Some Experiences of a Scholar-Collector," in *Building Book Collections,* p. 4.

43. I am indebted to William Stoneman, Florence Fearrington Director of the Houghton Library, for information and observations in this section. Telephone conversation, February 2, 2001. See also William A. Jackson, "Contemporary Collectors XXIV: Philip Hofer," *The Book Collector* 9 (1960): 151-52.

44. Ibid., p. 152.

45. Eleanor Garvey in *Grolier 2000,* p. 150.

46. Kenneth W. Rendell, *The Future of the Manuscript & Rare Book Business,* keynote address to the Antiquarian Booksellers' Association of America, April 17, 1999; published as an ABAA keepsake, p. [4].

47. "Special Collections and Academic Scholarship: A Tangled Relationship," in *Libraries and Scholarly Communication in the United States; The Historical Dimension,* pp. 68-69.

48. "American Book Collectors," p. 62.

49. Justin G. Schiller, *Digging for Treasure; An Adventure in Appraising Rare and Collectible Children's Books* (Indiana University, Friends of the Lilly Library, 6 November 1997), p. 3.

50. Elizabeth L. Johnson and Judith E. Endelman, "Lilly Library's Elisabeth Ball Collection," *AB Bookman's Weekly* (November 12, 1984), pp. 3417-18.

51. See Daniel J. Bradbury, "Barbarians Within the Gate: Pillage of a Rare Book Collection?" *Rare Books & Manuscript Librarianship* 9, no. 1 (1994): 8-18.

52. I am indebted to John Bidwell, Astor Curator and Department Head, Printed Books & Bindings, The Morgan Library, for information and observations in this section. Telephone conversation, January 4, 2001.

53. Wendorf, pp. 94-95.

54. Ibid., p. 98.

55. I am indebted to Andrea Immel, Cotsen Children's Librarian, Princeton University Library, for information and observations in this section. Telephone conversation, December 22, 2000; Cotsen Children's Library web site. Aug. 2, 2001 <www.princeton.edu/~cotsen/main>.

56. See William S. Reese, *The Rare Book Market Today*, pamphlet reprinted from the *Yale University Library Gazette* 76 (2000): 3-4. Aug. 2, 2001 <http://www.reeseco.com/papers/market.htm>; and Rendell, *The Future of the Manuscript & Rare Book Business*.

57. "How Shall I Leave My Books to a Library?" *The New Colophon; A Book-Collectors' Miscellany* (New York, 1950) [v.3], pp. 146-47.

58. See Clifford Lynch, "The Battle to Define the Future of the Book in the Digital World," *First Monday* 6, no. 6 (June 2001), section on "Continuity of Access and the Preservation of Our Intellectual Heritage." Aug. 2, 2001 <http://www.firstmonday.dk/issues/issue6_6/lynch/>.

59. Mary Douglas, "Foreword: No free gifts," in Marcel Mauss, *The Gift; The Form and Reason for Exchange in Archaic Societies*, translated by W.D. Halls; foreword by Mary Douglas (London: Routledge, 1990), p. vii.

60. See Natalie Zemon Davis, *The Gift in Sixteenth-Century France* (Madison, Wisconsin: The University of Wisconsin Press, 2000), pp. 3-10.